A Fixed
White Light

A Fixed

White

Light

Poems of Women Lighthouse Keepers

Suellen Wedmore

Down East Books

Down East Books

Published by Down East Books
An imprint of Globe Pequot
Trade division of The Rowman & Littlefield Publishing Group, Inc.
4501 Forbes Blvd., Ste. 200
Lanham, MD 20706
www.rowman.com
www.downeastbooks.com

Distributed by NATIONAL BOOK NETWORK

Library of Congress Cataloging-in-Publication Data Available

ISBN 978-1-68475-063-4 (paperback)
ISBN 978-1-68475-064-1 (e-book)

♾™ The paper used in this publication meets the minimum requirements of American National Standard for Information Sciences—Permanence of Paper for Printed Library Materials, ANSI/NISO Z39.48-1992.

For Syd

Marriage is four hands
tending the same fire

Contents

Acknowledgments

Thanks to the following journals for publishing these poems, sometimes in a slightly different form or with a different title.

Atlanta Review: "Learning Mantinicus Light"

Grayson Books: Proposing on the Brooklyn Bridge: "Under the Storm-Scraped Sky" (Formerly "What Does the Sea Care")

Grayson Books: Forgotten Women: "My First Rescue"

Folio: "Ailanthus Trees"

Hartskill Review: "Island: A Definition"

Lindenwood Review: "Pa Needed Me" (formerly "The Keeper of Black Rock Light.")

Louisville Review: "The Lighthouse Keeper's Wife"

Outrider Pres: Embers and Flames: "Midnight at the Top of the Tower"

Prism Review: "The Lighthouse Keeper Refuses a Boat to the Mainland"

Quill's Edge Press: Thank you for choosing the chapbook *Mind the Light* as a first-place winner in the 2016 annual contest. This work includes some of the poems in this volume, perhaps in another form or with a different title.

Sea to Sky Review: "Hurricane"

Serving House Journal: "None but a Donkey Would Call Saving Lives Unfeminine" (Formerly "I Can Handle a Boat")

PoetryJournal.com: "The Lighthouse Keeper's Wife, ""Becoming My Light'" (formerly "I Didn't Understand I Do"), "Learning Mantinicus Light," and "Journal: 1866"

San Pedro River Review: "The Lighthouse Keeper Refuses a Trip to the Mainland"

The Thacher Island Newsletter: "Polishing the Fresnel Lens"

Midnight at the Top of the Tower

Antimony, gum and starch
on tips of splintered wood—
lucifers* in a closed brass box,

these small sticks

a light keeper's defense
against an attacking gale.
I strike one across sanded paper

and a portrait of Blake's fallen angel

appears in the polished
lantern glass. Storm swallows sky.
Dark Prince, I carry your spark

to the lucern's waiting hemp,

unwavering then to the lamp's
concentric wicks,
attend it this long night,

a sign to my husband

and all those foundering at sea.
Devil's spark. Shiver of wood.
A small, good flame.

*Early matches were often called often "lucifers,"
 a term that persisted into the twentieth century.

Forgotten Women

In the last half of the nineteenth century, more than one-hundred women worked as primary keepers of our country's lighthouses. Twice as many were assistant keepers, and many more worked without pay or recognition in their husband's or in their father's names—this at a time when it was widely believed that the ideal woman was subservient to the men in her life, when society's expectations for women revolved entirely around managing her children and her home. An 1842 article in *Peterson's Magazine* titled "Education of Women" noted: "The province of women is to cheer our fireside, to educate our children. . . the business of men is to toil for the livelihood of those dear beings whom he has left at home, and to protect them against the evils of the world."

In the view of many, a woman's place was certainly *not* alone at midnight on the top of a lighthouse tower or in a skiff rescuing someone foundering at sea. And yet these hundreds of women worked in the physically and emotionally demanding role of lighthouse keeper, many of them alone, and some of them for most of their lives.

> Stench of right-whale oil,
> counting the stairs of winter:
> cramped calves, aching arms . . .

Were these women exceptional in their strength and endurance, or were they average women thrust into situations which nurtured heroism? And why did so many of them choose to remain in such demanding positions, year after year?

As a poet, I found myself trying to answer these questions, beginning with the biography of a local lighthouse heroine, Maria Bray. Left alone with a young nephew when her light-keeper husband rowed a sick assistant to the mainland, Maria kept the twin lighthouses of Massachusetts' Thacher Island burning for three storm-filled days and nights.

> This world wild with storm;
> I will be . . . of use.

* * *

I

Maria Bray

In the summer of 1864, Maria Bray accompanied her husband, Alexander, a wounded Civil War veteran, to his assignment as keeper of Cape Ann Light Station on Thacher Island, one mile off the coast of Rockport, Massachusetts.

A Mile from the Mainland

August is an unruffled sea,
        our skiff sliding down the ramp,
oars singing as we haul from silence

        to mainland's hustle, to buy milk,
calico and ribbon, a hoe, a sharp-edged axe.
        In the general store, I hold the day's

news in my hands: *Union Ships Sail*
        Past Mobile Bay, a poem
by Mr. Emerson on the front page.

        Come November, a day breaking pink
will depart in howling violet, and we order supplies,
        coal, beans and flour.

December is candlelight at four o'clock,
        in bitter-wind we scramble up
those many stairs, to feed the hungry lights.

The Lighthouse Keeper's Wife

A bitter storm had set in and there was Maria Bray, alone on
Thacher Island with her teen-aged nephew:1864
 — Cape Ann Museum, Gloucester, MA

My Husband stranded
    on the snow-blind shore
I tramp through sleet-

charged days,
shriek-sliced nights,
    climb 156 steps

to feed an insatiable
    child — this one
whimpering for

right-whale oil.
The sea heaps with foam,
    the northeast gale

white-crested
    as the storm that flung
the shipwrecked

Thacher children
like gulls' eggs
    against this island's

granite face.
  I do not eat —
what use is food?

  My world is oil
and wick, scouring
   the sooted

lantern panes;
  I'll not sleep
 until I hear

  above the surf
Alexander's easy
   Hollo!

Until I touch his face
  with my cracked
and frost-chafed hands.

Polishing the Fresnel Lens

— In 1864, the twin lights of Thacher Island were fitted with lenses developed by Frenchman Augustine Fresnel, which have been called "the invention that saved a million ships." Maria Bray would have assisted her husband in polishing these beautiful lenses.

I dress against the wind,
struggle toward the tower
to climb from island to sky,

> *How many were lost*
> *before Monsieur Fresnel*
> *sharpened light*
> *and tilted it toward the horizon?*

the metal floor
rings as my boot heel
strikes a rainbow,

> *Light splintered by the lens' prism*
> *into indigo, red, green and gold.*

Chamois in hand,
I stretch toward the lens,

> *a shimmering glass beehive*
> *taller than a man,*
> *mélange of diamonds and stars,*

swirl away night's soot.
"How does the lens work?"
a visitor once asked.

> *Imagine slicing a magnifying glass*
> *into a hundred concentric rings,*

each one thinner than the last,
so that it fragments
and refocuses the flame,

> *or imagine feathered light*
> *squeezed by great hands*
> *into a single beam,*
> *and hurtled toward the horizon.*

Journal, 1866

Island, I believed I could tame you
but when I cut a path
from house to garden
the earth exploded with pokeweed,

water hemlock, nettle.

*

Sunrise licks our bedroom walls....
but when I walk outside something new
    is insect-riven.

*

While I cut wild roses for our table,
a hawk devours a fledgling gull.

*

Summer's heat, winter's gale:
My Island, even January's
crisp diamonds belong to you.

*

Buried near the south trail:
the body of a child

drowned the day the *Watch and Wait*
was shaken and tossed
like so much loose change.

*

Pinnace and pirate, whale oil,
clay pipe thrust beneath a rock — here
yesterday's stories of
a capricious sea and fractured stones.

Questions

Why are you on this island?
> *Because I am a lighthouse keeper's wife.*

Why are you on this island?
> *A candle against the sky is pain's remedy.*

Why are you on this island?
> *Because only a soldier's wife*
> *understands the wounds of war.*

Why do you climb the tower every four hours?
> *For $950 a year, a barrel of salt pork, a peck of dried beans.*

Why do you climb the light tower every four hours?
> *Marriage is four hands tending the same fire.*

Why do you climb that tower every four hours?
> *Because disaster is only a gale away.*

Do you love the sea?
> *It is a drama of a thousand acts.*

Do you love the sea?
> *She is a treacherous friend.*

Do you love the sea?
> *She is fierce in vengeance,*
> *gallant in service,*
> *exacting in her splendor.*

Is an island a good place to raise children?

We learn from the terns' dives, the cleverness of gulls.
Is an island a good place for children?
  I fear for them, for the light tower is the first born.
Is this island a good place for children?
  In the island of my arms.

Would you choose to live on the mainland?
  This island is fifty acres of story.
Do you want to move to the mainland?
  Here is rhubarb, responsibility. Buttercups.
Will you retire to the mainland?
  To a cottage at the Atlantic's edge,
    my gaze toward the sea.

*   *   *

Alexander Bray, and Maria as his unpaid assistant, were keepers on the island for nearly five years. While Alexander died in 1885, Maria continued to live in Gloucester, Massachusetts, until age 93, where she was active in the Temperance Movement, became a leader of the Gloucester Women's Suffrage Association, and edited a local paper.

Reminiscence

I've known nature's moods, her rage and tantrums,
but three days and nights of howling wind
proved but drill for our fight for suffrage,
prejudice as bullying as
any nor'east gale.

II

KATE WALKER

. . . in sight of . . . the Torch of Liberty lived this sturdy little woman, proud of her work and content in it, keeping her lamp alight so that New York Harbor might be safe for ships to pass in the night.
— Obituary, *New York Evening Post: 1931*

A widowed mother of a young boy, Katherine Gortler immigrated from Germany to Sandy Hook, New Jersey, in the 1870s. Working in a boarding house, she met John Walker, the assistant keeper of Sandy Hook Light.

Loneliness:
long days, cold nights —
and here, a shy smile.

His offer to give her English lessons developed into a romance and they soon married. She learned to assist her husband in his lighthouse duties and delighted in caring for their vegetable and flower gardens.

Soon, however, John was promoted to keeper of Robbins Reef Light, anchored to a small ridge of rock and sand just off the tip of Staten Island. Gardening was out of the question.

*　*　*

Yearning Green

Nights, I dream of forest and fern, of bunchgrass
      waving in the wind. "Grün!" I say,
yearning the colors of my homeland.
      "Green, my dear: say *eeeee,*"
John coaches, but when I follow his advice,
      my tongue tangles with longing.

Some colors are easier to speak. *Rot.* Red,
      as in geraniums, tulips bursting into spring.
Violett. Violet. Heather across the valley
      of my childhood, as far as I could see.
Grau. The nearby sea churns this gray, threatening,
      cold. *Do you not hear loneliness*

as the surf rolls across the sand?
      I want to ask, but John's eyes
under the brim of his cap blink calm.
      I learn the names of trees,
flowers, kitchen utensils, and each day
      my hold on this new world grows.

"I will be keeper of Robbins Reef Light."
      John announces one day, pride in his voice
"Promotion. Say it, can you, my clever Kate?"
      "Pro . . . mo . . . grün?" My tongue trips
on this word. I have seen that light,
      naked on a rock in New York's Harbor.

Becoming My Light

— In 1885, Kate Walker reluctantly accompanied her husband to Robbin's Reef Light.

I.

gulls shriek

        I climb

slippery cold

        ladder rungs

to this light

        balanced

on a rock

        in New York's

howling harbor

        little Jacob

basket-lifted

        sways in

salt-charged air

        trunks thud

bang

        up uncounted

stairs

        to a bedroom

without curtains

        a bare floor

II.

The room reeks of coal and kerosene.
I won't unpack, I think —

what I want is geraniums, hollyhocks,
croquet on a plush lawn.

John lights the Aurora stove
and we lunch on molasses-sweet beans

with bluefish he caught
from the skiff

that rattles against
the surf-splashed tower.

III.

The next morning I climb
to the lantern room,
count a dozen ships

dependent on this light,
this keeper and his wife.
Looking up,

drifting clouds
whisper advice,
or perhaps none at all,

for what is fate
but what I choose
for tomorrow?

                    IV.

I place Mother's tea set
on a shelf
by the ever-kindled stove,

fold dresses into a cabinet
in the core of this

my lighthouse home.

Pneumonia

One day he spun me in muscled arms,

the next he fought for breath,

eyes sunk into his fine-boned face,

his lips, nailbeds blue, the skin

of his hands thinned and cracking.

whyhimwhymewhynowwhy I ask,

do you not see my child crying?

John is rowed to the mainland

in a flat-bottomed dory

never to return

and yet this lighthouse

stands through squall and hurricane.

After John

I.

I put on a pan of my husband's
favorite beans, simmered
with salt pork and onions,
serve them to little Jacob,
on the wide-board table
John made for us in Sandy Hook.

Grief with brown bread, butter.

II.

Nights I dream of ladders
   unfolding toward the sky
my skirt wind-kicked
   as I watch dolphins
scoop the sea,
   the platform below
blooming with forget-
      me-nots?

III.

John's words
   ride the rhythm

of the waves
                as I sweep stairs,
polish brass,
                trim wicks,
scour the lantern glass:
                Mind the light,
                Mind the light.

*   *   *

After John's death, several men were offered the post but turned it down because it was too lonely. When Kate applied for the position, objections were raised because she was only 4 feet, 10 inches tall and weighed barely 100 pounds. Time proved she was as good as any man, however, for she not only kept the light burning but rescued as many as 50 people in her 29 years as lighthouse keeper.

Hands

I wear mine
callused,
oak-hued,
nails trimmed
straight across,
scrubbed
with soap
I made myself
from wood ash
and lye,
the better
to row,
grapple,
carry and haul.
Should your skiff
run against
this rock-cleaved
tower,
you'll find
arms outstretched.
my grip firm!

Reminiscence

While my coal-fired stove lured
some from January's battering storms,
many came to drink tea with me
when the sea was smooth: summer
I was merry as they make 'em,
No matter the season, for thirty years
it's my light flashed
Welcome!

III

Abbie Burgess

. . . as the tide came in, the sea rose higher and higher, till the only endurable places were the light towers. If they stood we were saved, otherwise our fate was only too certain.

— Abbie Burgess, Letter to a friend: 1859

The oldest of four daughters, Abbie accompanied her family to Mantinicus Rock Light Station, twenty miles off the coast of Rockland, Maine, in 1853, when her father, Samuel Burgess, was appointed keeper. She was fourteen years old when she began to assist her father in his duties as lighthouse keeper.

Pa catches the boy
in me and something good
takes hold . . .

Mantinicus Rock, being far from the shore and the weather
being unpredictable, some years the supply tender was not able
to land with the family's provisions before winter weather set in.
In these times, Abbie's father would row to shore in a skiff, hop-
ing to soon return with food and medicine. Because her mother
was often sick, Abbie would act as lighthouse keeper and family
caretaker until her father returned. Most notably, at age 17,
Abbie acted as lighthouse keeper for three long weeks during the
gale of 1856.

*   *   *

Learning Matinicus Light

1853 — A New Home

I'm different here,
I say as Pa leads me
up the lighthouse stairs:

I've learned
that I am small,
the sea immense,

that this island's temper
changes with seasons
and tides.

I've seen whales
swim in families,
and gulls caring

for their puff-balled young.
Ships depend on us,
Pa explains, and

he shows me
how to trim wicks,
to fill the oil pan,

to light the fussy
Argand lamps.

Yesterday, I found

a sand dollar
washed up on the rocks
and tossed it back

into the watching sea.

1856 — *The Storm*

The Atlantic growls
        around my boot-clad feet
when Pa sails away to get supplies—

        Keep the light burning, he says.
Ma ailing, my sisters small and needy,
        and that night a storm comes

thumping, the surf pounds
        against the bolted kitchen door.
A wave crashes against the chicken coop,

        boards splinter and shingles fly.
Priscilla! I cry; my pet hen squawking
        as I race into the surge, gather her

in my arms. Charlene and Hope
        are next until all but one
are safe beside the stove,

        and when I look out again,
the hen house is gone.
        Those who imagine snow as white

haven't seen a northeaster,
            gray shrieking into blizzard-black,
the landing dock dissolved.

            I drag bedding up the tower stairs,
coax Ma and my fidgety sisters
            up the tower to the lantern room

where safety smells of whale oil
            and January cold.
We survive on eggs and corn meal;

            I fill the lamps every four hours,
scrape ice from the lantern glass
            with determined, mittened hands.

Under This Storm-Scraped Sky

even humpback and minkes
plummet to invisibility,
minutes stretch into hours,

days into weeks, and courage
unravels like fraying yarn.
What can I do

to stop the little one's
crying? Will Mother cough
throughout the night?

I should be satisfied with safety
while Pa jousts God
and wind changes, but when

I open the wicker basket,
starvation is but
a single egg away.

Island — A Definition

as in *surrounded by water,*
remote, as in *Mantinicus Rock,*
this our own tumble of stones —

*

a desert island is *abandoned,*
but what if it's home to just a few:
a man, his wife and children,
twelve chickens, cornbread in the oven,
beans on the stove?

*

Surrounded, as in *no way out,*
as when a fisherman drops a mackerel
into a school of sharks, the sea
glittering with scales,
a gray sky uncaring.

*

Isolated, as in feeling all alone,
as in reading March's newspaper in May,
a friend's letter delivered
a month after she had died.

Needle and Black Thread

Pa away on the mainland, of course,
when his fishing knife, in fidgety hands,
breaks my sister's fall, and I pluck

      her ear lobe

from a rock's crevice,
near the back of the house,
sculpt the ear whole again with Ma's
needle and black thread stitched

      into sea-iced skin.

We both cry, for who at seventeen
can play at God? And isn't
a lighthouse's promise of smooth sailing
presumptuous, when the sea prefers

      havoc over calm?

On the Island's North Hip

A little head ducked out from behind a cave-like opening near the
bottom of the rock, "Look at me, Abbie!"
— Abbie Burgess Lighthouse Heroine,
Sargent and Jones, 1969

where a slide of granite
leads to a cave, I descend
child-like
on my buttocks, relishing
the stones smooth
contours as I descend
onto pebbled beach,
each stone glistening.
My imagination
quickens — had Captain Kidd
stashed gold here,
to be discovered
on a return voyage?
Would I be rewarded,
as in my teacher's
Odyssey, with shelves
full of cheeses,
or be greeted by a one-eyed
giant with a taste
for humans, brains,
bones and all?
I step through the opening
when, from a crevice

in a nearby wall, not one
    but two eyes, brown,
soft as a doe's,
    gaze at me.
What is this big-eared creature,
    brown-fleeced,
cocooned in skin?
    Bat.
I'd not seen one
    here before —
web-winged,
    the only mammal
capable of flight.

Reminiscence

To board this island home,
twenty miles from friends, provisions, school;
our boat skimmed the rolling waves,
rode a six-foot breaker until
we were drawn so far onto rock
we could not be carried
back to sea.

IV

Catherine Moore

*Ours was the only light on the Connecticut side of Long Island.
Sometimes there were more than 200 sailing vessels in here at night,
and some nights there were three or four wrecks, so you can judge
how essential it was that they see our light.*

— *New York Sunday World: 1889*

The eldest of the three children of Captain Stephen Moore and
his wife Amelia, Catherine was twelve years old in 1817 when
the family went with their father to his appointment as keeper
of Fayerweather Lighthouse, at the mouth of Black Rock Har-
bor, Connecticut. Captain Moore had been injured years earlier

51

while unloading a ship and as soon as the family arrived on Black Rock Light, Catherine began assisting him with his work.

When her father's health worsened two years later, Catherine took over his duties entirely and remained the unofficial keeper until her father's death in 1871. Catherine is credited with saving 21 lives in her years as keeper of Black Rock Light.

Wish I'd saved
twice as many — and the half-dead:
I revived them when I could . . .

Finally, after her father's death, Catherine was officially appointed keeper of Black Rock Light — the job she had performed, unofficially, for 47 years. She remained at the station for seven more years, finally retiring in 1879 to a cottage with a view of Fayerweather Island.

*   *   *

Pa Needed Me

to trim the wicks: eight lamps
guzzling whale oil
might save a hundred ships

in fog-bound Long Island Sound;

at twelve I swapped dolls and jack stones
for this spit of land,
three acres and a forty-foot tower.

I was schooled by storm,

slept with my face turned
toward the lantern
should wind swallow the flames.

Our shelves were lined with books,

I sang land songs as I hoed our garden,
a geometry of peas and beans,
whittled eiders, ring-necks, mallards

from sea-tossed blocks of pine.

My playmates were chickens,
lambs, two Newfoundlands,
their fur scented with seaweed.

Now and then I rescued a fisherman,

hauled him in, fed him soup,
prayed he not die here
in front of our homely fire.

Shepherd, Abiding

A painting by Peter Paul Rubens, passed down through Catherine
Moore's mother's family, hung in the keeper's house.
— *Women Who Kept the Lights*,
Clifford and Clifford, 2001

Mr. Rubens understood us, I think —
    his *Shepherd with his Flock of Sheep*
hanging from a nail on our sitting room wall,

    the sheep, heads down, crunching grass,
the shepherd on a hillock gazing toward heaven.
    The artist hushed the nearby stream

with tiny brush strokes, the sky rising
    luminous from the horizon,
while above the shepherd a violet cloud

    swells with storm, an approaching
squall that will drive all to a distant shelter.
    Visitors seem troubled to see this work

in our simple, whitewashed home.
    Should be in the statehouse!
a mayor's wife declared

and when a selectman
    in a pressed suit scolded,
You dare keep this for your own!

I strode out the door, letting
it slam as I turned to the
un-accusing light tower.

Ailanthus Trees

When young Catherine Moore accompanied her father to Black Rock Light, she confronted an island of three straggly acres eroded by wind and storm.

— Women Who Kept the Lights,
Clifford and Clifford, 2001

Our wedge of world
gleams stony, cruel,
but here in my palm,

these winged seeds —

samaras, whirligigs,
spinning jennies,
will quickly root,

and this bald island

will be clothed in green,
bough, root, and owl.
There will be shade

for summer tea,

cool grass where
my Newfoundland
might nap, and come spring,

buds will open

into a gold chorus,
and unfurling leaves
will tame the wind

     off the cold Atlantic.

Fast-growing,
some call you
tree of heaven.

I plant and wait.

Syzygy

Today the moon, earth
   and sun aligned,
      gravity pulls the sea

away from our stolid planet
   revealing bleached shells,
      sea wrack, the bones

of an ancient ship.
   At sunset, when I stand
      barefoot at sea's edge

the surf will drive me back
   toward the time-worn tower.
      Surrounded by sea

I stand above it,
   yet, at sixteen, my blood
      runs on moon time —

the Monhegans
   call this bleeding time
      a blessing time;

I trust the waxing moon.
   Pa's potatoes, dug ripe,
      are tender, savory.

April, 1820

I pause on a knoll,
      seagulls wafting
spring's thermals
      when wind careening
from the northeast
      howls toward us
stinging bare wrists,
      an uncovered ankle,
leaves swirl
      from nearby scrub
and I stumble
      toward the tower's
spiral stairs,
      to kindle the wicks,
a signal to those
      uneasy
in this uncaring sea.

The Lighthouse Keeper Refuses
a Boat to the Mainland

Because my garden is fragrant
    with oregano and sweet bay,
    the tomatoes green
    and rain is on its way.
Because the sun rises over the Atlantic
    in a breathless shift
    from scarlet to blue,
because time on an island dissolves
    into sun, cloud, and star,
because here there is no need
    for polished shoes,
and there is grace
    in the headlong dive of gulls.
Because this tower
    is a torch
    against the black-hooded sky,
and the focused light
    of a Fresnel lens
    is hope for the lost.
    And who has not been lost.

Reminiscence

Who would dare
not call me "keeper"
when I stood at the top of this tower
year after year
feeding these lamps
so many gallons of pungent whale oil!

V

Ida Lewis

*When asked where she found her strength and courage, she replied,
"I don't know, I ain't particularly strong. The lord almighty gives it
to me when I need it, that's all."*

— *Notable American Women,*
James, et.al., 1971

Idawalley Zorada Lewis was 15 years old in 1857 when her
family moved to Lime Rock Light, off the coast of Newport,
Rhode Island, where her father had been appointed keeper.
When her father suffered a stroke, Ida and her mother tended
the light together.

Pa in his rocker,
unlit pipe in mouth, chewing
on our struggle....

After her father's death, her mother became ill and it was Ida alone who maintained the light station. She is reported to have saved 36 lives during her 39 years as keeper of Lime Rock Light.

*   *   *

My First Rescue
— 1869

That September day, I spied
the pitching catboat,
heard their laughter:
four boys about my age,

hooting, wrestling —
sons of Newport's finest,
judging by the boat, sleek
and shiny *Hug-Em-Snug*;

one boy shimmied up the mast
until, top heavy, the boat
plunged into the sea,
took on water until the hull,

frigid and so small only two
could grasp it,
rolled toward sky.
When the others, treading water,

screamed *Help! My God help!*
I jumped into my skiff,
rowed hard across the surf
until, beside them, stabilized

my boat, and drew them,
like Pa had taught me,
one by one across the stern,
hauled them back to our island,

to fireplace, blankets,
and Mama's molasses toddies.
Straw-haired Samuel, when
he opened his eyes, gushed

thankyouthankyouthankyou,
and yet on the mainland,
it would be twenty years
before he admitted

it was a keeper's daughter
who'd saved his privileged life.

Courage? Don't Know

but when I hear a cry for help
I jump into my skiff,
oars an outgrowth of my arms,
skim the gray foam,
slicing through the mad
Atlantic's peaks and troughs.

Last Fourth of July —
Ida Lewis Day, they called it —
Colonel Thomas Wentworth Higginson,
spoke for me (being audience shy),
thanking Newport for their gifts:
a boat with a red cushioned seat,

gold oarlocks, a silk pennant
which I hung on a wall
and forgot. Generous, though
I would choose to keep
those rescues to myself, the better
to remember who I am.

None But a Donkey Would Call
Saving Lives Unfeminine
    — *Harper's Weekly,* 1869

I can handle a boat
better than any man,
and should I hear
a call for help,
I pull a cape
around my poplin dress,
plunge into rain, snow,
gale's swirl,
to draw the nearly-drowned
across my stern,
struggle through surf
to haul them
to the warmth
of my island's
hip-roofed home.
Some laugh,
call me *unwomanly,*
and perhaps I am,
though Harper's Daily
chose my portrait
for this week's cover.

After Twenty Years Working Without a Contract,
Ida Considers Addressing the Superintendent
of Lighthouses

I.

Does it offend you, Mr.
Silk-Suspendered Pin-Stripe —

a reporter's admiration
for my accomplishments,

despite chignon,
scarf and petticoat, in the photo

in last month's *Evening News?*
Who's saved more lives

than me, and yet
I am rewarded with trinkets:

a medal, citations,
a skiff so awkward

I leave it tethered to a stone.
A man

would have a stipend
and a contract,

I serve, and yet,
please do not confuse

a sense of duty
with weakness.

II.

Last week I heard a scream,
jumped into my skiff,

rowed toward a soldier
foundering in the harbor,

pulled him over my stern,
thumped him on the back,

and sculled him home.
Heroic,

but not so difficult
as wrenching

prejudgment
from its unmarked channel.

Reminiscence

A light tower disciplines
hand and mind:
I trim wicks, erase soot,
but it was my skill with oars, soul taught,
that attracted our president's praise.
Tending a flame is learned –
saving lives is reflex
born.

VI

Barbara Mabrity

The undersigned inhabitants of Key West respectfully call attention . . . to the circumstances of Mrs. Mabrity, the keeper of the light upon this island, [who] has for a number of years performed the duties of her office with fidelity, and to the satisfaction of the Collector and of the Navigators . . .

—Key West citizens letter to
the Supervisor of Lighthouses, 1843

In 1826 Michael Mabrity was appointed keeper of Key West Light and his wife Barbara was named assistant keeper. The lighthouse being at the edge of the town, the Mabritys were spared the isolation of many light station appointments. Michael was even elected to the town council.

A Visit from Mr. Audubon

— Barbara Mabrity recalls conversing
with a traveling artist: April, 1832

I've named this — the most beautiful of woodland doves —
the Key West Pigeon, to honor you & your fine island!
declared the man with mud-caked trousers & startling brown eyes

sitting across from me, a tumbler of our own cool water in his
long fingered hands. He sighed. *Though I'm humbled*
rendering these, the most beautiful of woodland doves,

for capturing their colors in paint troubles me, I confess,
as it never has before. Though by last moon's rise —
(he sounded certain! this man with the startling brown eyes)

— I'd found a handsome carmine, for the pigeons' beaks, their eyes,
& had brushed a luminescence across the splendid heads
of these the most beautiful of doves, wired as

they were to convolvulus vines. I looked away then, musing
that I'd rather see our dove flying through mangroves
than captured by this man with startling brown eyes.

It's birds' liberty we envy, isn't it? That easy
lift from land to sky? He named this beautiful dove
the Key West Pigeon, before he killed
& wired it. The man with startling brown eyes.

Yellow

as in a lemon, an egg yolk,
a newspaper curled with age.
As in spineless, lily-livered,
creeping from swamp
to seize my husband,
handsome father of six,
cowardly, and yet it walloped,
nauseated, fevered him to bed,
blood flowing
from mouth and eyes,
his face the saffron hue
of the windows
of our own St. Paul's,
the promise of heaven,
or perhaps the flames of hell?
I am alone. I am alone.

*   *   *

*In the winter of 1832, Michael contracted yellow fever, a common
and little understood illness at the time. He died several weeks later,
leaving Barbara a widow with six children.*

> *Yellow Jack,*
> *that coward, fells*
> *my upright man.*

The Collector of Customs appointed Barbara to succeed her husband as keeper. In addition to caring for her family, her light-keeping record was flawless.

Spatterdock

My husband, you told me
    I could learn more
from a bird's call
    than from a shelf of books,
and now that you are gone

    I walk barefoot at swamp's edge
among the yellow pond lilies —
    spatterdock, cow lily, brandy-bottle,
where a great blue heron
    is poised, marble still,

its call scattering, like ash,
    discordant, until her chicks arrive
with their *chit-chit-chit* of hunger.
    The lilies' open like suns,
their overlapping leaves launching

    dragonflies into iridescent flight.
As spring's warmth seeps
    through my leather shoes,
I know I will stand once again,
    listening for the newly born.

*   *   *

Barbara Mabrity Maintained Key West Light through the hurricanes of 1835, 1841, and 1843 without incident — but in October, 1846, another heavy storm blew in, causing many people from the town to take refuge in the lighthouse. Barbara escaped the storm — perhaps by rescue from one of her grown children — and she continued her work as light keeper in a new, taller tower, constructed on higher ground, until 1864, when at age 82, she was fired, purportedly for daring to express Union loyalty in a Confederate stronghold.

Hurricane

This [storm of 1846] was the most destructive of any that has ever visited these latitudes.

> — Stephen Mallory, Collector of Customs,
> Key West, Florida

An iguana sunning on a rock sensed it first —
    the water in my storm-glass plunging,
so I invited neighbors into the safety of my light tower.
    Waves twice my height thundered ashore,

the water in my storm glass, plunging, plunging,
    I promised: *She's a survivor, this brickwork tower.*
Steeple-high waves thundered ashore,
    the wind roared like a fire gone wild.

She's outlasted three hurricanes, this brickwork tower!
    I promised, though schooners splintered across the reef
and the wind-rattled tower shook like a giant's toy.
    Trees storm-flung against the tower stuck fast;

vessels sank, bottoms up, while inside the tower
    a mother, crying, pressed her infant against her chest.
Chickens storm-flung against the tower stuck fast
    and little Mariann sucked her thumb and whimpered.

Pinch that baby's cheek, someone cried. *My God, is she all right?*
    The tower quieted in storm's eye, growled at wind's return,
little Marianne covered her ears and whimpered.
    Stone, earth, brick and sand yielded to waves crash,

the tower groaned as it was dragged out to sea;
      an Iguana sunning on a rock had sensed it first.
There's a white-sand beach where the light once stood —
      I had invited neighbors into the safety of my tower.

My Husband, Now I Climb

alone each night
        to tend
these sulky
        lamps,
polish reflectors,
        certain
as I have become of
        uncertainty,
Do you remember the
        Isaac Allerton
laden with cargo,
        families
seeking a new home,
        passengers
dashed as they dared
        these coral-
spiked shoals?
        Did you
hear that Sarah
        Margaret Fuller —
who once announced
        A woman
can be anything
        she chooses —
drowned in a shipwreck
        off Fire Island,
the lighthouse there
        squat

and weakly lit? Some
      clear day,
will you approach
      and call
my name? Nights,
      you know me:
a fixed white light,
      keeper
of the harbor.

Reminiscence

What is more difficult, tending
six children or fifteen lighted wicks?
Nature corralled my days: floods, wind, hurricane,
while this steadfast lens
coddled me
through my eightieth year!

Notes

Forgotten Women (p.13)
The number of women lighthouse keepers is based on the handwritten "Lighthouses, Keepers and Assistants," Volume I–VII, located in the National Archives Record Group 6, Entry 92. (as reported in *Women Who Kept the Lights*: Second Edition, Mary Louise Clifford and J. Candace Clifford: Cypress Communications, 2001).

Maria Bray (p.15)
Photo courtesy of the Cape Ann Museum, Gloucester, Massachusetts.

Polishing the Fresnel Lens (p.19)
Augustine Jean Fresnel invented a superior lighthouse lens, first tested in France in 1823, which eventually came to be used in most of world's lighthouses. This lens captures more oblique light from the source and focuses it so that it is visible from great distances.

Kate Walker (p.27)
Photo by Isaac Almstad, 1900, collection of the Walker family.

Pneumonia (p.33)
Five years after the Walkers arrival, John became ill with what was at the time called "winter fever. There was no treatment for this disease, which was the third major cause of death in this century.

Abbie Burgess (p.39)
Image courtesy of the Coast Guard Archives.

Learning Matinicus Light (p.41)

Despite the popularity of the use of the Fresnel Lens worldwide, most lights in America continued use of the Argand Lamp until the 1850s or '60s. This outdated lamp demanded more of the keeper's time, feeding it, trimming its wicks, and polishing it and its parabolic reflectors. The Argand lamp output was estimated at seven candlepower.

Needle and Black Thread (p.46)

The incident of sewing up a child's ear with black thread, which could have happened on Matinicus Light during the long absences of Abbie Burgess's father, was actually recorded in the history of keeper Kate McDougal of Mare Island Light Station, California from 1881–1916.

On the Island's North Hip (p.47)

This poem was inspired by an exploration of a grotto-like cave on Maria Bray's Thacher Island. The reference quoted from *Abbie Burgess: Lighthouse Heroine* convinced the writer that such cave-like structures might be found at low tide on many islands.

Catherine Moore (p.51)

Author's portrait of Catherine Moore as a young woman.

Haiku (p.52)

The words are taken from Catherine Moore quotes published in *Women Who Kept the Lights: Second Edition*: Clifford and Clifford (Cypress Communications) Alexandria, Virginia: 2001.

Ida Lewis (p.63)

Photo ca. 1912, courtesy of the Library of Congress.

Reminiscence (p.71)

Among the many visitors to Lime Rock Light who praised Ida Lewis's dedication and accomplishments were U.S. President Ulysses S. Grant and Elizabeth Cady Stanton.

Barbara Mabrity (p.73)

Author's painting of Barbara Mabrity standing before the Key West Lighthouse.

A Visit from Mr. Audubon (p.74)

On April 30, 1832, Audubon wrote in the journal he kept during his time in Key West: " . . . we steered toward the mangrove, mud up to our knees, baking and broiling, and finally reached the lighthouse." It is this writer's belief that a man as curious as Audubon would have been interested in the workings of the light, and that Barbara, being self-reliant and spunky, might have had her own opinion on Audubon's work.

There is a recorded narration, supposedly in the "voice" of Barbara Mabrity in the Key West Lighthouse Museum, which states that her children met Audubon when" he was invited to dinner,' indicating that a first meeting of Audubon and Barbara Mabrity family might have been only one of many.

Audubon's dialogue in the poem is taken from the journal he kept during his visit to Key West.

Yellow (p.75)

There were several outbreaks of yellow fever, which can be transmitted by the bites of the Asian tiger mosquito and the yellow fever mosquito, in early Key West. At the time the only recommended treatment was quarantine.

Hurricane (p.79)

Early reports after the hurricane of 1846 reported that Barbara

* * *

Mabrity had been the only survivor of the collapse of the Key West light Tower, and that all five of her children had died at the time. It is now generally believed, however, that newspapers had confused the collapse of Florida's Sand Key Light Tower (where an entire family did perish) with Key West's light. Local historians generally believe that although Barbara did invite her neighbors into the safety of the light tower, one of her adult children, sensing the danger, brought her to his or her home at the time the hurricane dragged Key West light into the sea.